Puppy Training

An Essential Guide for Everything You Need to Know To Train A Perfect Dog.

By

Kevin Parker

Contents

Introduction

People believed that dog training consisted only of teaching dogs obedience precepts, which was frequently accomplished via harsh punishment. It was seen as a luxury for pet owners, and it was sometimes mistakenly assumed to be something so easy and basic to do that anybody could do it without the assistance of a professional.

That view still exists to some extent, but dog owners are rapidly realizing that, although this profession of dog training is unregulated, finding the appropriate trainer to assist them and their dogs in the correct path and give much-needed assistance may be life-saving.

Understanding how your dog learns and using positive training techniques to make training as rewarding, effective, and simple as possible is one of the greatest ways to create a healthy connection with your dog. Punitive trainers think that the best way to create so-called 'balance' with your dog is to show her who is in charge by being her alpha or pack leader. Because the tactics utilized to achieve this dominating position are physically and mentally harmful to your dog and hazardous to you, this technique is bound to fail from the start. Constructive training, in which a dog is rewarded and motivated for positive conduct, helps you build a connection with your dog focused on mutual trust and respect rather than fear and intimidation.

From the minute you bring your puppy home and begin to house train it, you will be instructing it. Puppies begin learning from the moment they are born, and competent breeders begin petting and socializing as soon as possible. As soon as the puppy can open its eyes and walk, some training may begin. Although puppies have short attention spans, you may expect them to learn basic obedience cues like "sit," "down," and "stay" as early as seven to eight weeks of age.

Formal dog training has typically been postponed until the age of six months. In fact, this is a very inopportune moment to begin. Every encounter teaches the dog something new, and postponing training means the dog will lose out on chances to learn how you want him to act.

Consistency, tolerance, and positive thinking are essential while housetraining your dog. The idea is to develop positive behaviors and a loving relationship with your pet.

A puppy's training takes about 4-6 months on average, but it may take up to a year in certain cases. The sizes may be used as a predictor. Smaller breeds, for instance, have smaller bladders and greater metabolisms, necessitating more frequent excursions outdoors. Another factor to consider is your puppy's past living situation. You may need to assist your puppy in breaking bad behaviors in order to create better ones.

One of the most enjoyable aspects of owning a pet is proper training. When done correctly, you can ensure your pup's happiness, affection, and safety for a lifetime. Down, stay, and sit commands not only assist your dog in cooperating at home, but they may also help them be a decent canine member outside of it.

This book is a complete guide on puppy training and teaching your puppy the basic commands.

Chapter 1: Why Do I Need To Train My Dog?

People believed that dog training consisted only of teaching dogs obedience precepts, which was frequently accomplished via harsh punishment. It was seen as a luxury for pet owners, and it was sometimes mistakenly assumed to be something so easy and basic to do that anybody could do it without the assistance of a professional.

That view still exists to some extent, but dog owners are rapidly realizing that, although this profession of dog training is unregulated, finding the appropriate trainer to assist them and their dogs in the correct path and give much-needed assistance may be life-saving.

Science has progressed, and the field of dog training has flourished as a result, but not without debate. The ever-growing legion of awakened positive trainers, such as

Victoria's worldwide VSPDT dog trainer network, has challenged the careers of many conventional trainers who continue to preach antiquated dominance and punishment-based ideologies. As a consequence, dog owners are faced with a more difficult decision when selecting a dog trainer.

What is no longer debatable is that, if you choose a skilled, really positive trainer, whatever money invested in training will be multiplied in terms of a good relationship and a peaceful home for both you and the dog.

The truth is that the vast majority of dogs in private ownership have had no official training, positive or negative. Because dogs are increasingly sharing our homes and lives, it is more crucial than ever to provide every dog with proper canine education. Thousands of dogs will be saved from being relinquished to shelters because of behavioral difficulties that may have been avoided. Taking the effort to train your dog can make life simpler for both you and her, and it may even save her life.

Five Reasons Why Your Dog Should Be Trained

1. To Establish A Good Relationship

Understanding how your dog learns and using positive training techniques to make training as rewarding, effective, and simple as possible is one of the greatest ways to create a healthy connection with your dog. Punitive trainers think that the best way to create so-called 'balance' with your dog is to show her who is in charge by being her alpha or pack leader. Because the tactics utilized to achieve this dominating position are physically and mentally harmful to your dog and hazardous to you, this technique is bound to fail from the start. Constructive training, in which a dog is rewarded and motivated for positive conduct, helps you build a connection with your dog focused on mutual trust and respect rather than fear and intimidation. Those who can impact their dogs' behavior without using violence and gently work through any issues are the most successful instructors. Positive reinforcement-trained dogs are more patient, self-controllable, and act more consistently in a variety of scenarios.

2. To Instructs Life Skills

Every dog must learn how to live happily in a domestic setting. Domestic dogs may seem to have an easier existence than their wild counterparts; however, living in a human environment comes with its own challenges. Teaching your dog basic manners and giving her adequate mental and physical stimulation can help her avoid anxiety and other stress-related behaviors like destructive chewing, excessive barking, and aggressive behavior. Setting your dog up for success by regulating her surroundings and making it simple for her to succeed is a key component of the learning process. Understanding how your dog reacts in different circumstances is the first step. For instance, if your dog is very outgoing and enjoys meeting new people, train her to welcome them without leaping or overpowering them when they enter your house. This helps her control her excited behavior while yet enabling her to appreciate the coming of the new individual. Put your dog there behind the baby gate and in her own room while new people come if she is apprehensive or afraid of them. This will help your dog remain stress-free and emotionally stable. For dogs that are socially inexperienced or scared, space is critical, and controlling your surroundings to minimize pressure ensures everyone happy and secure.

3. To Boost Sociability

Enhancing your dog's social contact delight will give her the courage she needs to cope with the stress of home life. It takes time and effort to teach your dog appropriate manners and behave in various settings, but persistent dedication assures success. Our dogs are held to high standards, and we encourage them to be nice to everyone they encounter, even if they're uneasy in certain settings. As a result, it is critical to socialize your dog by providing her with positive experiences in the company of a diverse range of people, animals, and places. Doing so at an early age will instill confidence in her and reduce the likelihood of her having anxiety and discomfort later in life. Your dog does not have to contact another dog or a human to be socialized physically. Humans constantly socialize without physically touching one another. It's just as vital to training your dog to tolerate physical contact as it is to expose her to varied circumstances where she may watch and 'converse' at a distance. Individuals are naturally attracted to engage with an adorable puppy, and when dogs meet one other, there is a good chance that physical contact will occur. It's all about keeping your dog comfy in these social settings but also making sure she's not forced into something she doesn't want to be in. Do not feel obligated to push your dog to engage with people if she does not want to. Like humans, not all dogs are friendly. Recognizing how your dog copes will influence how far you can go; although having a friendly dog is preferred in our community, keeping your dog out of an uncomfortable environment is not a failure. Observing her coping strategies can help you appreciate and comprehend her limits.

4. To Stay Away From Problematic Behaviors

Training your dog develops a communication language between you and your dog that fosters comfort and security. The more time you spend educating your dog on living effectively in a human environment, the fewer undesirable behaviors will arise due to a lack of understanding. Unfortunately, many dogs are penalized for bad behavior that might have been prevented if more time had been spent helping them learn. Many dogs react well to commands like sit and stay in the classroom, but they are unprepared to cope with life's stresses in the real world. Make sure that each signal or action has a purpose. Sit is a beneficial cue since it may be used before opening the door or crossing a road, whereas coming enables your dog to be off-leash while still teaching her to return to you when needed. Hand targeting or the contact cue, for instance, not only allows your dog to become accustomed to hands being outstretched towards her, which she will likely encounter many times during her life, but it also helps teach a recall.

5. For Companionship and Loyalty

Positive thinking does not exclude you from correcting your dog's misbehaviors; it only means that the "discipline" should be utilized as constructive counsel rather than as a threat. Discipline in time outs, removal, verbal interrupters, or ignoring undesirable behavior is significantly more successful than violently repressing it. Assisting your dog in making the correct decisions and knowing what she needs to be happy can strengthen your relationship.

There seems to be a widespread notion that optimistic trainers never say no to their dogs or let them get away with bad conduct. There's also a myth that positive trainers educate by cramming food into dogs' faces and that they lack the ability to treat serious behavioral behaviors like aggressiveness.

Positive training assists individuals in fostering connections with even problematic dogs by identifying and reversing problematic behaviors without resorting to force or fear. This alters behavior without jeopardizing the relationship between the dog and the owner. Anyone may use incentives to teach dogs to learn, but changing undesirable behavior without using force requires significant knowledge and experience.

People who devote time to training their dogs have happier relationships with their canine friends. Your dog's success will be determined by a good mix of learning etiquette, boosting sociability, and providing her with the appropriate kind of outlets. People who do not provide their pets with the necessary training are doing them harm and will face issues in the future. The learning process does not have to be expensive or time-consuming, and the more pleasurable it is for both of you, the better.

Chapter 2: Puppy Behavior and Training

When Should I Begin Training My New Puppy?

From the minute you bring your puppy home and begin to house train it, you will be instructing it. Puppies begin learning from the moment they are born, and competent breeders begin petting and socializing as soon as possible. As soon as the puppy can open its eyes and walk, some training may begin. Although puppies have short attention spans, you may expect them to learn basic obedience cues like "sit," "down," and "stay" as early as seven to eight weeks of age.

Formal dog training has typically been postponed until the age of six months. In fact, this is a very inopportune moment to begin. Every encounter teaches the dog something new, and postponing training means the dog will lose out on chances to learn how you want him to act. The dog is starting to cement adult behavior patterns and go through fear phases throughout the adolescent stage. Puppy-hood behaviors may need to be modified. Furthermore, everything that has been erroneously learned or educated will need to be rectified and retaught. Puppies can learn a lot from a young age.

"A technique known as food-lure training may be used to teach puppies the commands 'sit,' 'down,' and 'stand.'"

Use strategies that concentrate on positive reward and gentle instruction when starting training at 7 to 8 weeks. Puppies' attention spans are limited. Thus practice sessions should be quick yet frequent. Using a technique known as food-lure training, puppies may be taught to "sit," "down," and "stand." We persuade the dog to follow its nose into the appropriate positions for "down," "sit," "stay," and "stand" by using food goodies.

What Is The Best Way To Get Started With Food Lure Training?

Small treats or a favorite toy may be used to encourage your puppy to do most activities. By displaying the puppy the reward, issuing a command, and relocating the reward to elicit the appropriate reaction, the puppy may be persuaded to deliver the desired reaction if the reward is sufficiently tempting. Food propped up over the puppy's nose and gradually crept backward should elicit a 'sit' reaction; food drawn down to the ground should elicit a 'down' reaction; food brought back up must elicit a 'stand' response; food expected to hold out at a distance should elicit a 'come' response, and food retained at your thigh while walking should elicit a 'heel' or 'follow' response. The puppy should quickly understand the meaning of each command by coupling a command phrase with each action and rewarding each acceptable answer.

How Frequently Should I Issue The Command?

Ideally, you should only say the command phrase just once and put the puppy into positions with your food. Add in verbal praise and a loving pat after the puppy has completed the activity called secondary reinforcers. If the puppy doesn't instantly respond to the initial order, you are probably moving too rapidly. If you keep on repeating the instruction, the puppy will understand that it can wait for multiple repetitions before obeying. If the puppy does not follow, keeping a leash on might assist you in getting a quick reaction." If you keep on repeating the command, it will eventually work.

"The puppy will understand that a lot of repetitions are necessary. Before anything has to comply, it must be acceptable."

Remember that your puppy does not understand the meaning of the term until later in the training process. As a result, you might teach your puppy to sit just as readily with the word banana (or seat in some other language) as with the word sit. The idea is to link the word, in this example, "sit" to the action of putting one's rear end on the ground.

How I'm Going To Get Rid Of The Lure And Food Incentives?

You'll start by letting the puppy see the foodstuff in your hand so you can get her focus and use it to lead her into position. As your puppy's obedience improves, you may begin to conceal the food in your hand while still giving the order and repeating the action or signal she has learned to obey. The puppy will soon start to anticipate a reward every time she completes the assignment. Then signal and deliver the order, but only praise her and give her a loving pat after completing the duty. Then you may start varying the frequency by praising with "excellent dog" and maybe stroking each time, but providing the food at random intervals, such as every three or four times. The puppy should eventually react to the hand gesture or the order.

The words "good dog" and an appreciative pat become secondary reinforcers over time. They take on more importance and become reinforcement in and of themselves because they have previously been connected with food. As you'll never always have food around you when you need your pet to comply, it is critical to apply secondary reinforcement. Furthermore, if you depend on food to convince your puppy to obey, you will end up with a dog that will only do the duty if you reward him.

"Over time, the phrases "good dog" and other acts of love serve as additional reinforcers."

Training begins with a range of family members in specified periods throughout the day. You should reserve all of your awards for these training sessions. However, after time, you should start asking your puppy to execute the duties at different times.

How Much Time Must I Devote To Teaching My Puppy Daily?

You do not have to work out in a scheduled session every day. Rather, include these things into your daily routine. At least fifteen minutes of training every day is a target to aim towards. These sessions might be as little as 5 minutes and spaced out throughout the day. Make sure that everyone in your household asks your dog to do these activities. Always remember to practice in every part of your home. You want your dog to "sit," "lay down," and "stay" throughout the house, not just at the training center. Practice in all places where you want your puppy to act and feel at ease in the future.

"To have a well-trained dog, you must first be well-trained yourself, and you have to be devoted to reinforcing the training tasks."

For the first year of your puppy's life, you should feed him daily.

As you begin to introduce the puppy into your life, use these training practices. Ask your dog to "sit" before you give her food, "sit" before you allow her out or in the door, and "sit" before you touch her, for instance. These are the instances when your puppy is much more likely to obey because he or she wants something. In this manner, you're always teaching your dog throughout the day while also setting predictable norms and routines for encounters and assisting the dog in learning who has control of the resources. It is advisable to train your puppy before obtaining each needed essential in order to avoid complications. Allowing your puppy to sit before receiving food or a reward eliminates begging, and training your dog to sit before opening the door reduces leaping up or bolting. Be inventive. To have an adult dog, the effort you invest in teaching your puppy now will pay dividends. You must be devoted to repeating the training activities on a nearly daily basis during the first year of your puppy's life in order to have a well-trained dog. The more you train and oversee your puppy, the less likely it is to engage in inappropriate behavior. Dogs do not self-train; if left uncontrolled, they will behave like dogs.

What Should I Do If My Dog Is Too Preoccupied Or Excited To Be Controlled?

Training should start in a peaceful, distraction-free area. The incentive should be very compelling so that the puppy's attention is completely focused on the trainer and the incentive. A beloved toy or a special dog treat may be more tempting than a tiny food reward, which is usually the best option. It's also a good idea to teach the puppy just before a planned mealtime when it's the most hungry. For challenging or stubborn pups, leaving a leash connected and using a head collar for extra control is the best approach to assure that the puppy will execute the required activity and react correctly to the order. If the puppy does not instantly respond, you may use this method to urge it into the proper reaction, and the pressure may be removed as soon as the intended reaction is reached.

When Should I Start Introducing My Puppy To Other People?

Social interaction should commence as early as you adopt your puppy, which is usually around the age of seven weeks. During the socialization stage, which lasts between 7 and 14 to 16 weeks, puppies instinctively accept new individuals, different species, and new settings. This period allows for a plethora of introductions, many of which will result in wonderful memories that will last a lifetime. During this time, puppies are eager, adventurous, and unrestrained, so take advantage of their excitement. During this time, be careful to safeguard your puppy and make sure that all of his or her encounters are good, enjoyable, and are not fear-inducing.

Chapter 3: House Training Your Puppy

Consistency, tolerance, and positive thinking are essential while housetraining your dog. The idea is to develop positive behaviors and a loving relationship with your pet.

A puppy's training takes about 4-6 months on average, but it may take up to a year in certain cases. The sizes may be used as a predictor. Smaller breeds, for instance, have smaller bladders and greater metabolisms, necessitating more frequent excursions outdoors. Another factor to consider is your puppy's past living situation. You may need to assist your puppy in breaking bad behaviors in order to create better ones.

And don't panic if you have setbacks during training. They'll learn as long as you keep up a management program that involves bringing your puppy out at the first indication of having to go and rewarding them.

When Should You Start House Training?

 According to dog experts, House training for your puppy should begin between the ages of 12 and 16 weeks. They have quite enough control over their bladder and bowel functions at that stage to learn to retain them.

Housetraining may take longer if your puppy is elder than 12 weeks once you bring them home and has been urinating in a cage (and maybe ingesting their waste). With encouragement and incentive, you'll have to change the dog's behavior.

Housetraining Techniques For Your Puppy Experts advise limiting the puppy to a certain area, such as a crate, a room, or a leash. You may gradually offer your puppy greater freedom to walk about the home as they learn that they need to go outdoors to do their business.

Follow These Steps To Begin House Training:

- Feed the puppy on a consistent schedule and retrieve their food in between meals.
- Take the puppy out for a potty break in the morning and then every 30 minutes to an hour after that. Also, after they finish a meal or wake up from sleep, take them outdoors. Make sure they go out before they are left alone at night.

- Keep an eye on them outdoors, at least until they're housetrained.
- Praise or reward your dog when he or she eliminates outdoors. A wonderful reward is a stroll around the neighborhood.

Housetraining A Puppy With A Crate

In the near term, a crate might be an excellent option for housetraining your puppy. You'll be able to keep an eye on them for signals that they want to go outside, and you'll be able to educate them to hold till you open their crate and let them out.

Here are some pointers on how to use a crate:

- Make sure it's big enough for the puppy to stand, roll around, and lay down in, but not so huge that they can go to the bathroom in a corner.
- If you're going to leave the puppy in the crate for more than 2 hours, make sure he gets fresh water, ideally in a dispenser that you can connect to the crate.
- If you cannot be at home throughout the house training phase, make sure that someone else provides them with a mid-day break during the first eight months.
- If your puppy is urinating in the crate, don't use it. Eliminating in it might indicate a number of things: they may have picked up undesirable behaviors from the shelter or pet shop where they previously resided;

they may not be receiving enough exercise; the cage may be too small, or they might be too young to keep it in.

Indications That Your Puppy Wants To Eliminate

Complaining, circling, smelling, barking, or yelping or scratching at the door if your puppy is unconstrained are all indicators that they need to go. Remove them as soon as possible.

Setbacks In House Training

Puppies up to a year old are prone to mishaps. Accidents may occur for various causes, including insufficient house training or a change in the puppy's surroundings.

Continue to teach your dog even if he or she has an accident. If it still does not seem to be working, visit a veterinarian to find a medical problem.

Potty Training Your Puppy: Dos And Don'ts

- While housetraining your puppy, remember to keep do's and don'ts in mind:
- Punishing your dog for an accident is never a good idea. It instills terror in your pet.
- If you find your puppy doing anything wrong, clap loudly to let them know they've done something wrong. After that, call them outdoors or gently grab

them by the collar. Praise them or offer them a tiny reward when they're done.

- If you find proof but don't witness the act, don't become angry and shout at them or rub their nose in it. Puppies aren't capable of making the connection between your rage and their mishap.

- Staying with your puppy outdoors for extended periods may assist in reducing accidents. They could need additional time to explore.

- Instead of using an ammonia-based cleaner to clean up messes, use an enzymatic cleanser to reduce smells that may encourage the puppy to return to the same location.

Chapter 4: How To Potty Train Your Puppies

Puppy pads and paper training provide a temporary solution to housetraining, but crates are an essential puppy housetraining item that may make your life simpler.

Housetraining requires consistency, care, understanding, and tolerance.

One of the most crucial initial steps you can take for a happy, healthy life together is understanding how to toilet train puppies at the appropriate time and location. One of the most common causes for dogs losing their homes or ending up in shelters is house soiling. Few individuals are ready to put up with a dog who ruins carpets and floors and creates a nasty mess to clean up after a long day at work.

That's why it's critical to do a preliminary study on how to house train a dog, determine what would work best for your scenario, and devise a strategy.

To train your puppy, there are 3 tried-and-true approaches.

- Paper training
- Crate training

Walking outdoors regularly is also beneficial.

According to Dr. Burch, each has advantages and disadvantages, but they may all be effective if you follow a few fundamental guidelines, such as:

- Managing your dog's nutrition.
- Maintaining a constant routine for going outdoors, feeding, and exercise.
- Getting regular exercise—aids motility.
- Reminding your dog that "going outside" is a good thing.

Let's take a closer look at some of these ideas.

Crates Are A Popular Potty Training Tool

Many individuals who are new to dogs are uncomfortable with the concept of restricting their pups in a crate, but this aversion usually fades after a few days of living with a new pet. Crates for dogs make life simpler. For various reasons, such as vet appointments, travel, healing, and protection, it's a great idea to get your dog used to one.

Dogs are den creatures, and whether you offer one or not, they will seek out a little canine shelter for protection. As a result, teaching your dog to appreciate her kennel is pretty simple.

The idea behind utilizing a cage for housetraining is that puppies are very clean animals that don't like having a urine-soaked mat in their living place anymore than you do. The crate must be just big enough for the dog to lay down, take a stand, and roll around in. If it's too big, the dog will think it's okay to eliminate in one corner and then contentedly lie down away from the mess. Many crates include partitions, allowing you to change the size as the puppy develops.

The puppy will generally let you know when she has an urge by whimpering and scratching. That's her indication that she has to go and is ready to leave her little cave. Right now! Don't wait because allowing your dog to lose control in her cage will teach her that it's okay to trash her living place. Then she'll have no qualms about dropping tiny packages all-around your neighborhood.

Paper Training And Puppy Pads

The usage of paper training and puppy pads, according to Dr. Burch, maybe "tricky" since "you're encouraging two distinct possibilities for the puppy." Puppies would learn to hold it inside and only excrete in designated areas outside in an ideal environment. However, certain situations may need creative thinking, such as a person with work that prevents them from returning home numerous times a day or a smaller dog living in a harsh winter climate. Puppy pads allow a dog to relieve herself in a designated area at home. After the dog has matured, the owner may work with her to have her do her business outside all of the time.

Make A Schedule For Your Puppy's Housetraining

It is critical to the success of housetraining. Puppies' bladders are small, and water passes straight through them. The solid stuff is the same way. You must ensure that your puppy has sufficient opportunities to do the right thing.

According to a decent general rule, dogs typically control their bladders for hours equivalent to their age in months up to roughly nine months to a year. (Keep in mind, though, that anybody can't hold it for more than 10 to 12 hours!) It is reasonable to anticipate a 6-month-old puppy to be able to carry it for roughly 6 hours. Always keep in mind that each puppy is unique. Therefore, the timeframe may vary.

When creating a timetable, keep track of everyday occurrences and your puppy's routines. You should anticipate taking a puppy out:

- When you wake up in the morning
- At the end of the day
- After drinking
- When you've finished playing inside
- After a period of confinement in a crate
- When you wake up after a nap
- After chewing a bone or a toy
- After eating

In 24 hours, you may be dashing to the piddle pad or street a dozen times or more. If you work, establish some form of plan to preserve that schedule (take your dog to work or hire a dog walker). You'll be able to put this messy section behind you faster if you can convey the concept that there is an acceptable spot to the toilet and that other locations are off-limits.

Supervision And Observation

You must keep a close eye on your puppy for specific signs and rhythms. Some pups may be able to retain it for a longer period than others. Some will have to leave the house if they play or become aroused. Some will stop during a play to urinate and then continue playing. Canine bathroom habits are very distinctive, much like human kids'.

Dietary Control

Puppies' digestive systems are still developing, so they can't tolerate a lot of food. As a result, it's suggested that you divide the puppy's feeding schedule into three little meals. Another consideration is the food, which should be of the greatest possible quality. Make sure that anything you pick is acceptable to your dog.

The easiest technique for a dog owner to determine if it's time to adjust his or her dog's food is to examine its feces. If your puppy's feces are persistently thick, loose, and smell, it's time to speak to your veterinarian about moving to a different diet. Overfeeding may also cause diarrhea, which can make housetraining even more difficult.

Praise

Scolding a dog for soiling your carpeting, particularly after it's happened, would just make her believe you're crazy. Similarly, some archaic punishment tactics, such as rubbing a dog's nose in its poop, are so odd that it's difficult to conceive how they came to be or whether they ever worked for anybody. Praise a puppy for doing the correct thing; on the other hand, it works the best for everything you will accomplish together in your life. Every time she does this basic, natural deed, make her believe she's a little canine. Cheer, applaud and toss cookies to show your appreciation. Let her understand that no other achievement has ever been as significant as this pee—not traveling to the moon, breaking the atom, or making coffee. Give your dog one of his favorite treats as a reward. Make sure they're little and simple to digest for your dog.

Dr. Burch advises that if your dog has an incident, you should not make a big deal about it and instead clean up the mess. The aroma will be removed using a cleanser that eliminates smells, so the dog would not use it again. Before cleaning the carpet, blot up any liquid on the carpet.

If you see your dog squatting to pee or defecate, grab her up and take her outdoors right away. Give her love and attention if she accomplishes the task outside. When it relates to housetraining, remember that prevention is key.

Problems with Housetraining

Following these guidelines will almost always result in a puppy that is well-trained in the home. But things don't always go as planned.

House soiling might be an indicator of a physical problem, according to Dr. Burch. "A dog that has proven tough to housetrain should have a thorough medical workup well before the multiple month mark," she advises. If your dog is healthy, the very next step is to contact a trainer who has dealt with similar situations before.

Here are some of the most frequent issues trainers have heard:

1. "My lapdog has pooped all over the place!" This is a regular occurrence among owners of toy dogs. Some trainers suggest training little dogs to utilize indoor toilet places in the same manner that cats do with litter boxes. There are also genuine dog toilet boxes for indoor usage, in addition to piddle pads. Others claim that if you are consistent, you can house train a small dog. It may just need a bit more time, focus, and effort.

2. "My dog continues peeing in the same location where she peed the last time she had to have a crash." That's most likely because you didn't wipe up the mess well, and there's still a residual odor, indicating that this is a good toilet site. Make sure you have lots of pet stain enzymatic wipes in your new puppy supply package, and carefully read the directions on using them.

3. "I let her have free reign of the flat. There was shambles when I got home." This is a typical error made by dog owners. They perceive early evidence that the dog is grasping the concept and claim success prematurely. Keep to the program even if the puppy is continuously performing what you want. This will ensure that the beneficial behaviors are established.

4. "He is soiling his crate!" Dogs who arrive from pet shops, shelters, or other settings where they have been kept for lengthy periods and have had no option but to defecate in their kennels will frequently soil their crates, according to Dr. Burch. Going back to step one with crate and potty training is the best way. The steps are as follows:

- Evaluate your dog's urine and bowel control while he is not in the crate.
- Maintaining a strict diet and regimen.
- Allow for regular visits outdoors, such as after each meal, the initial thing in the morning, and the last thing at night.
- Consider hiring a dog walker if you work.
- Remove any smells by cleaning everything thoroughly.

How Long Does It Take To Potty Train A Puppy?

According to Dr. Burch, this may vary greatly. Maturity, learning history, as well as your approaches and consistency, are all elements to consider. The development of an 8-week-old puppy differs significantly from that of a 5-month-old dog. After just a few days, some pups have excellent manners. Others may take months, particularly if the dog came to you from a less-than-ideal circumstance.

Chapter 5: Puppy Feeding Fundamentals

You may easily get overwhelmed if you go down the dog food section of any big pet supply store or visit the shelves of a specialty pet food store. This is particularly true for puppy owners, particularly first-time dog parents. When did it become so difficult? Dog food selections were significantly more restricted back in the day, and even responsible owners didn't give a hoot about what poured into their dog's bowl.

The process may have become more complicated, but that's a good thing. Higher-quality nutrients, superior sourcing, and customized food formulae all contribute to our pups' overall wellness. Understanding your puppy's specific dietary requirements is just as crucial as knowing what to give him.

Because every puppy is different, please visit your breeder or veterinarian if you have any questions or concerns regarding your puppy's diet, feeding regimen, or nutritional health.

"How long must I feed puppy meals?" many dog parents question. Here's a rough guide of what your puppy will need at each step of his first year.

A First-Year Timeline for Feeding Your Puppy

- At **6- 12 weeks,** Puppy food, a diet particularly prepared to suit the nutritional demands for proper growth, should be offered to growing puppies. Adult food deprives your puppy of essential nutrients. Nutritional requirements are normally met with four feedings each day. By 9 or 10 weeks, large breeds should be offered unmoistened dry food, while tiny dogs should be given by 12 or 13 weeks.
- At **3 - 6 months,** Reduce the number of feedings from four to three per day during this time. By 12 weeks, a puppy's potbelly and pudginess should be gone. Continue to give puppy-size amounts until her body type develops if she's still roly-poly at this age.
- At **6 -12 months,** start feeding twice a day. Spaying or neutering reduces energy needs significantly; move from nutrient-rich puppy diet to adult maintenance diet after the procedure. Small breeds may shift at 7

to 9 months, whereas larger dogs may do so at 12, 13, and even 14 months.

- After the age of 1, most owners give their adult dogs 2 half-portions of food every day

How Much Food I Should Feed My Puppy?

When it comes to canine feeding, there's an adage that goes, "Watch the dog, not the dish." Portion sizes should be determined by body condition rather than the quantity eaten or left in the dish. Portion sizes are determined by an individual's metabolism and body shape, and nutritional needs differ from one dog to the next. Don't be concerned if your puppy misses meals or picks at his food. It might indicate that she is ready to stop eating or that you've given her too much food; in any case, just lessen the amount supplied.

Also, if you're teaching your dog with treats, make sure you alter the quantity you provide at meals. When using rewards for training, make the reward as little as possible.

How Frequently Should I Feed My Dog?

Puppies, like human newborns, need many tiny meals every day of a diet made specifically for their nutritional needs. The majority of dogs, but not all, complete their meals rapidly. Feed at regular intervals and in regular quantities to prevent fussy eating habits, and don't keep food out for longer than 10 - 15 minutes.

Your breeder, as well as your veterinarian, will be a great source of information on both of these topics.

Is It Better To Give Them Dry Food Or Wet Food?

Many pet food manufacturers have collaborated with canine nutritionists to create unique formulae for big and small-breed pups.

- Canned food is the most costly to provide, but it is also the most appealing to dogs. However, be wary of "all-meat" promises. To meet nutritional needs, your dog should eat a comprehensive, balanced diet. It's possible that meat alone won't enough.
- One-serving packages of semi-moist food are available. It's frequently shaped like a hamburger.
- The most cost-effective option is kibble, and the main manufacturers provide a full and balanced food for dogs of all kinds and ages. Dry food may be consumed directly from the bag.

Some dog owners believe that hard kibble has an oral hygiene benefit because its friction helps keep the teeth and gums healthy. Water or canned food may be used to wet kibble. Although optional, this addition may improve the taste of the food.

Keep Track Of Your Puppy's Growth And Weight

- Print and online growth and weight charts are available. Weekly weigh the puppy and keep track of his growth, comparing him to breed-specific weight charts. To attain an average rate of growth, adjust his food consumption.
- It's simple to weigh a dog, even a wiggling puppy. Simply weigh yourself before and after handling the dog. Subtract the difference to get the weight of the puppy. And that's it!
- Don't be concerned about an oz. or two in any direction; no two dogs, even the same breeds, are developed the same way.
- A young dog that is overweight is more likely to develop orthopedic issues due to the stress placed on underdeveloped joints. Obesity may also lead to diabetes, heart disease, other organ disorders, and overall fatigue.

Tidbits For Puppy Feeding

- Feeding your dog as soon as you return home may cause separation anxiety in your dog. A more pleasant approach to say hello is via play or grooming.
- You may get canned or dried prescription diets from vets to feed dogs with renal illness, cardiovascular disease, diabetes, and other severe diseases when

medically required. Without a prescription, these items should never be consumed.

- Certain vitamins or mineral supplements (like excess calcium provided to a large-breed dog on a balanced diet) might do more damage than benefit when used inappropriately.
- Consult your vet and, if feasible, the breeder before making a big adjustment in your dog's food. Once you've decided on a formula, stick to it. Sudden changes in meals might cause digestion issues.
- Carrot or apple slices in small quantities are healthy, low-calorie treats that most dogs like.
- There should always be fresh water accessible. Consider putting up additional indoor/outdoor water stations throughout the summer. Wash the water dish every day to reduce bacteria accumulation.

Advice On Puppy Nutrition

Verify that everyone is on board.

The feeding schedule for your dog must be adhered to by everyone in your family. If someone in your family has a soft spot for a giveaway, your dog will discover it and exploit it, undermining the good you're trying to accomplish. Keeping a dog in good shape requires a concerted effort from everyone on the team.

Is It Okay To Give A Dog A Bone?

Our best suggestion is to proceed with care. Cooked bones of any form, including poultry and pork bones, are prohibited. They fracture into shards, causing choking and significant injury to the dog's mouth, esophagus, and intestines. If bitten into little bits, any bone may obstruct the intestines and induce severe constipation, cause bruising to the mouth and vital organs, or lodge in the throat, resulting in death. It's crucial to keep in mind that bones have very little nutritional value.

There are alternative options for satisfying a dog's chewing needs. Dogs of all sizes can chew on commercially available chewing toys and imitation bones.

"First, we eat," said M.F.K. Fisher, a renowned culinary writer. Then we take care of the rest." This is also true for our dogs.

Chapter 6: Mouthing, Biting, and Nipping in Puppies

Puppies spend a lot of time eating, playing, and discovering new things. Puppies use their jaws and needle-sharp teeth in all of these regular activities. Puppies often chew, mouth, or bite on people's hands, limbs, and clothes while they play with them. When your puppy is 7 weeks old, this type of behavior is lovely, but when he's 3 - 4 months old—and growing larger by the day—not it's so adorable!

What To Do When Your Puppy Starts Mouthing

It's critical to assist your puppy in learning to control his mouthy behavior. This lesson may be taught in a variety of methods, some of which are better than others. The ultimate objective is to teach your dog to quit biting and mouthing others. However, the most crucial goal is to educate him that people's skin is very delicate. Therefore he must use his mouth with care.

Bite Inhibition: Teach The Puppy To Be Careful

Bite inhibition is a term that describes a dog's capacity to regulate the power with which he bites. While a puppy or dog hasn't been taught to bite restraint with humans, he doesn't understand the delicacy of human skin and bites too hard, even when playing. Some behaviorists and instructors feel that if a dog has trained to use his mouth softly while dealing with humans, he will be less likely to bite violently and break skin in situations other than play, such as when he is fearful or in pain.

Bite inhibition is frequently learned when pups are playing with other dogs. When you watch a bunch of pups play, you'll notice that there's a lot of chasing, ganging up, and wrestling going on. Puppies bite each other all over the place. Occasionally, a puppy may bite his companion too hard. The victim who has been bitten yelps and typically quits playing. The yelp typically catches the perpetrator off guard, and he or she stops playing for a brief while. However, both teammates are soon back in the game. Puppies learn to manage the severity of their bites via this kind of contact, ensuring that no one is wounded and the game may continue uninterrupted. Puppies may learn to be kind to others, and adults may teach them the same lesson.

Allow your dog to mouth on your hands while you're playing with him. Play with him till he bites very hard. When he does, let out a high-pitched shriek and let the hand go limp, as if you're harmed. This should surprise your puppy enough to have him quit mouthing you for the time being. (If yelping doesn't appear to work, say "Too bad!" or "You botched it!" in a severe voice instead.) Reward your dog for coming to a halt or licking you. Carry on with whatever you're doing before. Yelp again if your dog bites you forcefully. Within a 15-minute interval, repeat these instructions no more than three times. You can use a time-out approach if yelping alone doesn't work.

When it comes to preventing pups from mouthing, time-outs are generally highly helpful. Yelp loudly when your dog delivers a powerful bite. Take off your hand when he is frightened and comes to look at you or glances about. Either overlook him for 20 - 30 seconds or get up and go away for 20 - 30 seconds if he begins fobbing on you again. Go to your puppy after the brief time-out and urge him to interact with you again. It's critical to instill in him the understanding that pleasant play continues, yet painful play must come to an end. Play with your pup until he begins to bite hard once again. When he does, go through the steps again. You may tighten up your restrictions a little after your puppy isn't biting as fiercely as he used to. Make it a point to train your pup to be even nicer. In reaction to fairly hard bites, yelp and pause the game. Continue howling and then ignoring or putting your pup in time-out for his most venomous bites. Repeat for his next-hardest bites, and on and on, till your puppy could play with your hands very softly, modulating the power of his mouthing so that you feel very little pressure.

Instruct Your Puppy That Teeth Are Not Appropriate For Human Skin

- If your puppy attempts to munch on your toes and fingers, substitute them with a toy or chew bone.

- When rubbed, caressed, or scratched, puppies often mouth on people's hands (unless they're sleeping or preoccupied). If your puppy becomes agitated when you touch him, use your other hand to distract him by offering him little goodies. This will assist your puppy in becoming used to being touched without biting.

- Instead of wrestling and aggressive play with your hands, offer noncontact games like fetch and tug-of-war. Put tug toys in the pocket or have them conveniently available once your dog can safely play tug. You may quickly divert him to the tug toy if he begins mouthing you. When he seems like mouthing, he will start anticipating and looking for a toy.

- Carry your puppy's preferred tug toy in the pocket if he bites your ankles and feet. When he traps you, cease moving your feet right away. Take the tug toy out of the bag and wave it around enticingly. Begin to move again as soon as your dog takes the toy. If you don't have the toy on hand, just stop and wait for the dog to stop biting you. When he comes to a complete stop, praise him and treat him with a toy. Rep these techniques until your dog is comfortable watching you walk around without chasing your ankles or feet.

- Make sure your puppy has lots of fascinating and fresh toys to play with instead of chewing on you or your clothes.
- Allow your puppy lots of opportunities to play with other pups and vaccinated dogs. Interacting and socializing with other dogs is beneficial to your puppy's growth, and if he spends a lot of his time with them, he'll be less tempted to play rough with you. Prefer enrolling your puppy in a reputable puppy class, where he will be able to socialize with other pups while also learning new abilities.
- Be patient and considerate. Playful mouthing is typical behavior of a puppy or dog.

General Precautions

- Do not tempt your puppy to play by flapping your toes and fingers in his face or smacking the sides of his face. If you do these things, your puppy may become more likely to bite your feet and hands.
- In general, do not dissuade your puppy from interacting with you. A dog and his human community form a deep relationship via play. Rather than not playing at all, you want to train your puppy to play gently.

- When your puppy mouths, don't yank your feet and hands away from him. This will make him want to reach out and grasp you. It's much more useful to let your hands go slack so that they're no longer enjoyable to play with.

- Slapping or striking pups for mouthing is likely to make them bite harder. They frequently respond by being more aggressive in their play. Physical punishment may make your puppy fearful of you, and it may even lead to genuine hostility. Scruff shaking, whipping your puppy on the nose, forcing your fingers down his mouth, and any other penalties that might injure or terrify him should be avoided.

When Does Mouthing Turn Into Anger?

The majority of puppy mouthing is normal. Some pups, however, bite out of panic or frustration, and this form of biting might indicate future aggression issues.

"Temper Tantrums" In Puppies

Puppies throw temper tantrums from time to time. Tantrums usually occur when a puppy is forced to perform something he dislikes. Even something as simple as holding your dog still or touching his body might agitate him. Tantrums may also occur as the game progresses. (Even human "puppies" may have tantrums when they are too enthusiastic or agitated during play)! A puppy outburst is more severe than fun mouthing, although distinguishing between the two may be difficult. In most circumstances, a playful puppy's face and body are relaxed. His snout may seem wrinkled, yet his facial muscles do not seem to be tense. Your puppy's body may seem rigid or frozen if he is having a rage tantrum. He could growl or draw his lips back to reveal his fangs. His bites will almost always be much more severe than usual mouthing during play.

Avoid yelping like you're injured if you're holding or managing your puppy, and he begins throwing a temper tantrum. This might cause your puppy's violent behavior to persist or worsen. Instead, maintain a cool and emotionless demeanor. Don't injure your puppy, but if you can, keep him in a tight grip without tightness until he stops trying. Allow him to depart when he has quieted down for a minute or two. Then make arrangements to get assistance from a knowledgeable specialist. Biting in frustration regularly is not something that a pup will grow out of. Thus your pup's behavior should be evaluated and corrected as soon as possible.

Chapter 7: Important Puppy Commands To Teach Your Puppy

One of the most enjoyable aspects of owning a pet is proper training. When done correctly, you can ensure your pup's happiness, affection, and safety for a lifetime. Down, stay, and sit commands not only assist your dog in cooperating at home, but they may also help them be a decent canine member outside of it.

We've compiled some most important dog commands to train your furry pet initially. Basic instructions are taught first, followed by more complex techniques.

2 to 3 times a day, for 10-15 minutes at a time, rehearse all of them with your puppy. It should take your pup a few weeks to become used to it, but once they do, you will be set for life.

Sit

1. Hold treat above your dogs head
2. Move it behind their head until they sit
3. Repeat

The most basic command, "sit," will be useful regularly. "Sit" is a go-to command whether you have visitors or your dog is receiving a reward.

Hold a goodie in your hand and place it over your dog's head to teach him to "sit." Slowly slide it behind their heads, then say "sit" and praise them when they crouch.

Watch Me

1. Hold a treat near your dog's nose

2. Slowly move it towards your face saying "watch me"

3. Repeat

"Watch me" is a lesser-known yet crucial command. If you bring your puppy to a crowded place, this advice will come in helpful. You'll realize when to use this command as you come to know your dog better - some dogs require it when automobiles pass by, rodents run in front of them, and so on.

To start training for "watch me," just hold a goodie near your dog's nose. Then, carefully pull the reward closer to your face, stopping when it's close to your nose. Say "watch me" and give your dog a treat.

Down

1.	Put strong-smelling treat in front of your dog
2.	Make sure they smell it
3.	Move the treat down to the ground

"Down" is a difficult command to teach but one that your puppy will benefit from knowing. It's not just adorable, but it's also useful for when your puppy gets a bit too enthusiastic.

Hold a strong-smelling goodie in front of your puppy and let them sniff it. Bring the reward to the floor after they've done so, and your puppy will ultimately follow. Say "down" and give them the reward when their belly would be on the floor.

Stay

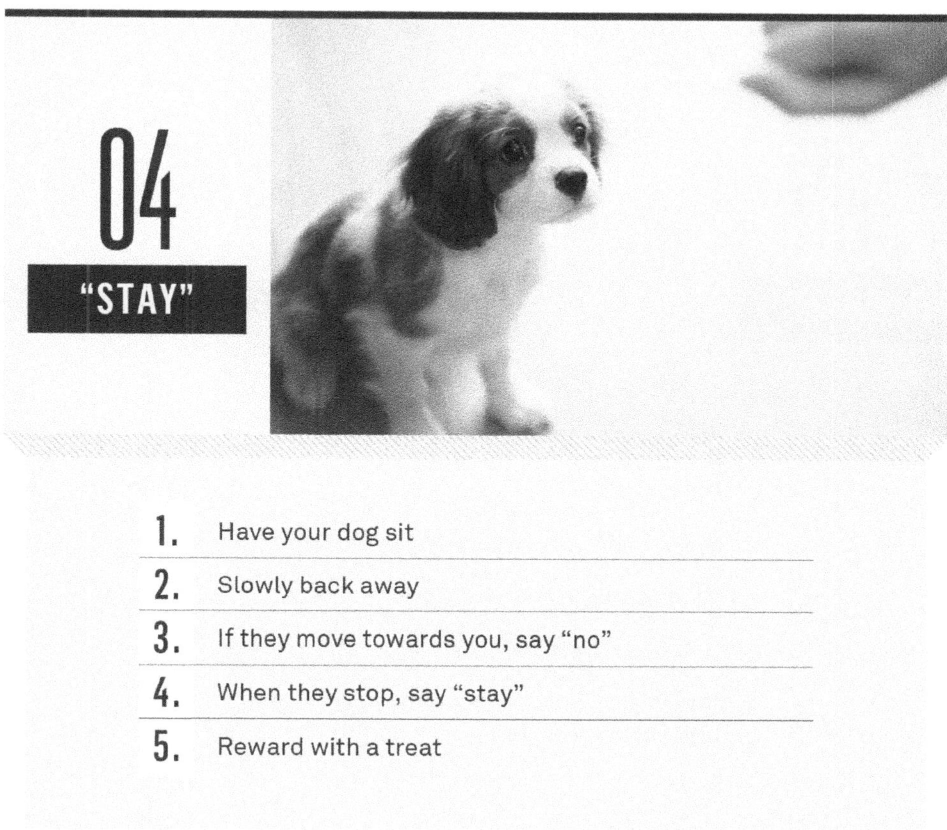

The most crucial command to teach your puppy is "stay," which will be useful regularly. Stay must be taught at a young age for their safety and the protection of others.

Begin by teaching your puppy how to sit. Then take a step back from your puppy. If he or she approaches you, say "no" and ask them to sit. Speak "stay" when they come to a halt. Then provide a prize and tell them to "come."

Wait

1. Have one person outside the door, one inside
2. Person outside opens the door
3. If the dog moves towards them, shut the door
4. Reward with a treat when the dog doesn't lunge at the open door

"Wait," like "stay," is a phrase that is used when someone enters your house via the front entrance. Your puppy will most certainly become excited whenever someone enters your home, regardless of how well behaved they are, but it's critical that they don't run into you or your visitors.

It's important to train your puppy with two humans to teach him "wait." One should go outside your home, while the other should remain inside with your puppy. The person on the other side of the door should open it. When your puppy approaches the door, the one on the inside must say "wait" as the one on the outside shuts the door.

Rep this process as needed, rewarding your puppy when they don't approach the door.

Chapter 8: What Breed Is Right For You?

What are the best dog breeds for families? What are the most suitable dog breeds for children? It might be tough to select which dog or puppy is the best match for your family when introducing a new pup or dog to your household. We've compiled a list of the top 5 dog breeds for families with children.

Labrador Retriever

Personality: Outgoing and friendly

Good with kids: Yes

Energy Level: Very active

Weight: Male (65-80 pounds), Female (55-70 pounds)

Height: Male (22.5-24.5 inches), Female (21.5-23.5 inches)

Shedding: Regularly

Barking Level: Medium

Life Expectancy: 10-12 years

Trainability: Desires to satisfy others

Bulldog

Personality: Calm, brave, and pleasant; dignified yet amusing

Good with Kids: Yes

Energy level: Not so much active. Bulldogs don't beg to be played, but they do need daily walks and the occasional romp.

Weight: Male (50 pounds), Female (40 pounds)

Height: 15-16 inches

Shedding: Seasonal

Barking Level: Quiet

Life Expectancy: 8-10 years

Trainability: Response Well

Golden Retriever

Personality: Friendly, intelligent, and devoted.

Good with Kids: Yes

Energy Level: Active; This dog is energetic and active. Need regular exercise.

Weight: Male (65-75 pounds), Female (55-65 pounds)

Height: Male (23-24 inches), Female (21.5-22.5 inches)

Shedding: Seasonal

Barking Level: Only Barks When Necessary

Life Expectancy: 10-12 years

Trainability: Desires to please others

Beagle

Personality: friendly, curious, and Merry

Good with Kids: Yes

Energy Level: Active; This energetic, quick, and compact hound pet requires plenty of exercises

Weight: 20-30 pounds

Height: 13-15 inches

Shedding: Seasonal

Barking Level: Loves To Be Vocal

Life Expectancy: 10-15 years

Barking Level: Loves To Be Vocal

Pug

Personality: charming, Even-tempered, loving and naughty

Good with Kids: Better with supervision

Energy Level: Pugs are somewhat active; they aren't natural athletes, but they possess powerful legs and an insatiable curiosity, so they should be exercised regularly.

Weight: 14-18 pounds

Height: 10-13 inches

Shedding: Regularly

Barking Level: Barks only when necessary

Life Expectancy: 13-15 years

Trainability: Agreeable

Conclusion

Understanding how your dog learns and using positive training techniques to make training as rewarding, effective, and simple as possible is one of the greatest ways to create a healthy connection with your dog. Punitive trainers think that the best way to create so-called 'balance' with your dog is to show her who is in charge by being her alpha or pack leader. Because the violent tactics utilized to achieve this dominating position are physically and mentally harmful to your dog and hazardous to you, this technique is bound to fail from the start. Constructive training, in which a dog is rewarded and motivated for positive conduct, helps you build a connection with your dog focused on mutual trust and respect rather than fear and intimidation.